Born Ugly

Volume no. 1

Born Ugly
Poems, prose, & Nonsensical Inter-workings

By Cody Conrad

New Flesh Press • NFP: #03

First Printing: 2015

ISBN: 978-0-692-38444-2

Cover photo by Logan Lettiere
Cover design by Cody Conrad
Edited by Logan Lettiere

New Flesh Press
Portland, Oregon & Phoenix, Arizona

www.newfleshpress.com

newfleshpress@gmail.com

For those who stuck around.

Authors note

A common misconception and myth of writing, art and the creative right brain is that it is best from a place of darkness, malice, hardness, manic behavior and absolute shipwreck. I have recently found it to be quite the opposite. The best work is done in victory or in spite of these shortcomings, feelings and thoughts. What now will follow within these pages are examples and experiments of such.

Introduction

This collection of work spans through the turbulent years of 2012 to 2014 and is my way of putting to rest the ghosts that have followed me for those shaken years. It's about dealing with personal ambivalence and attempting to step into my own bag of skin.

This book is a tombstone to what once was and a step forward to what will be.

Cody Conrad

Born Ugly

Prayers to the Deaf

Sleep well, sleep well
But know you'll never dream
Suspended in disbelief
By the old rugged cross
You sang but never did see

Upside down, hanging from the tops
Of agnostic trees
The wild animals tearing limb from limb
With no savior or hopes to be released

Held in a moment of clarity
As I remember I never prayed for the angels
And the angels never prayed for me

As a child I could hear the notes
I could even pluck the strings
But as Jesus wept for his people
I couldn't hear the harmony

Death of a Fellowship as a Young Man

I wish to speak to the ghosts
Of those who have now
Long since strayed from my life
We intersected to never expect to split
Paths move on.

Stitching the seams is tiresome and tedious
So instead I'll visit the places we cherished
As you will too
But those paths and moments will not cross again.

Basket of Flowers
(Molded and Melting)

She cried for summer's air
He cried for winter's sting
Yet in the end what they wanted
Was the same thing

He was never brave
Her mind was a swamp
When they mended together
It was all they could want

The light was let in
But he pulled away
She wanted to taste substance
He just couldn't stay

The freedom of nothing
Meant more than words could say
He died that day
It all was just feign

Cody Conrad

IMSOSICK
OF THIS FACE.

Born Ugly

        I am confident
in my
        over all lack of
confidence.

Cody Conrad

Poems written from the Northwestern trains and PDX MAX
08/13 – 10/13

Born Ugly

(Written aboard the trains throughout Portland, OR.)

_____Fills The Void

Do you lie awake with these thoughts too?
Of autumn days sewn together yet
Seamlessly tearing us apart.
And the thought you miss our city
Just like I miss it too.

These days it's the mutter of your voice
That rings in my ears like violent tinnitus.
In dreams the sting of its ring becomes song
And it's all I can ever manage to sing.

But in the end its the a piercing prodding of silence
That pokes at my fears.
The grave in its grace is so profound
And now I am deaf, just torn to death.

(Written aboard the trains throughout Portland, OR.)

Swollen Vessel

A thousand miles
And no place to rest my head
Yet here I am sleeping,
Living, residing
In this empty chest.

But if home is where the heart is
Then I have no bed.

This heart remains homeless
And I am still tied
And docked
You forgot,
Then you fled.

Born Ugly

(Written aboard the trains throughout Portland, OR.)

Worse Than Alone

Lost my head in the oven
When you took this thumping muscle in a jar

Now it beats resting on your mantel
Hands reaching, lungs deflate
But I laugh from afar.

(Written aboard the trains throughout Portland, OR.)

Bottle, Swallow, Bravery

The devil in your ear
Worms crawling through your chest

A mimed angel in a bottle
A twitched tongue and words slip

Your vision is clogged
Your balance askew

Several ounces later
Another body gone
Another nailed numeral.

Born Ugly

(Written aboard the trains throughout Portland, OR.)

Sometimes I really do not know whether it'll be these white knuckles or time that will get me in the grave quicker.

Just come quickly.
Don't cease to take me.

Cody Conrad

(Written aboard the trains throughout Portland, OR.)

Young and Lust

Don't say you'll go
This house was never a home

Don't say you'll stay
I am better off alone.

Born Ugly

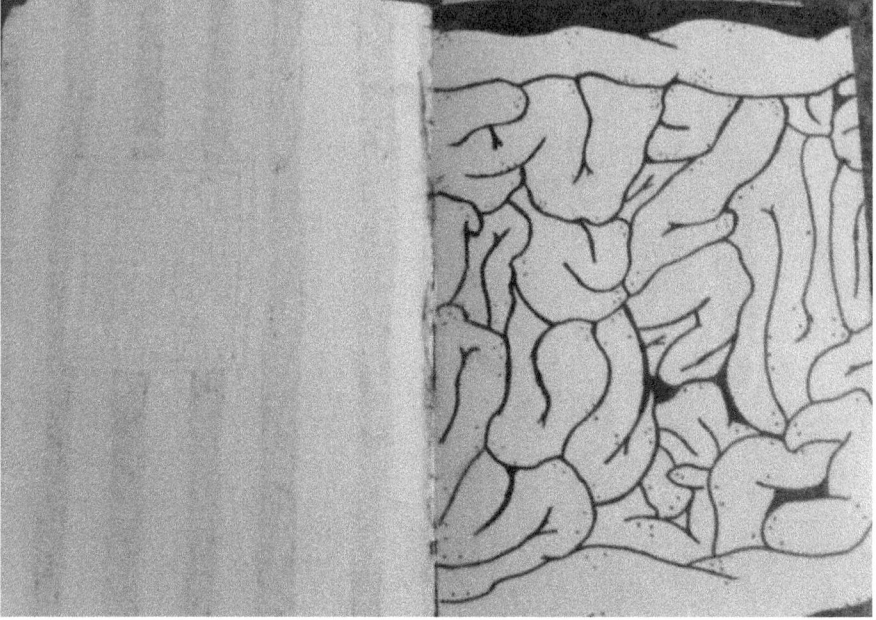

Basket of Flowers pt. II

She is a star I can barely see
One I can never touch
My love was there
It just was never enough

Born Ugly

Drawing Into The Net

We enter this world alone
And we leave just how we came
In Heaven are we given hands to hold?
Or just a headstone with a name?

Flowers grow the graves
Of the blameless and unlawfully maimed
They too left the world
Just how they came

In our blessed Kingdom
Are we given faces?
Thoughts, analogue limbs, and voices?
Or does it end how it began
A tunnel of blackened purity
Dirt amongst the ashes.

Old Ideas

My mind travels in spurts to old avenues
A simple search for the honey drip of familiarity
Instead bitterness lingers
On the tongue, teeth and cheeks
As I trip and stumble
Passing only vacancy or the homes of ghosts.

Uncontrollable urges to walk down old avenues
And see the faces I hardly can forget
Hear the tones and melodies of vibrating vocal chords
The drum beat of footsteps
The horn section of laughter

Every day gives birth to new old avenues
Something more to long for
And a body to miss
I sing the songs of yesteryear
Nostalgia is a prison
Memories are a home

Born Ugly

Young Old Soulless Soul

Jesus save me
Bhudda teach me
G-d punish me
Allah bless me
Reiki heal me
Saṃsāra reincarnate me
The Tao harmonize me
Emptiness confuse me

Cody Conrad

Born Ugly

You think you're an artist
I think I am one too
So does everyone else

Limestone Carver

Lets celebrate at the slaughter
With cake, tea, and laughter
That our faces were given numbers
That there is no ever after

For who holds together our bones
Fragments in unison alone
And he to who marks the grave
Needs his name written on a stone

So give thanks to the date given
That we own a day of living
Many years spent behind us
Still posses the same day of ruin

Dirt In The Ground

Born in dirt is where I come
And here within the dirt
Is where I come un-done

Cody Conrad

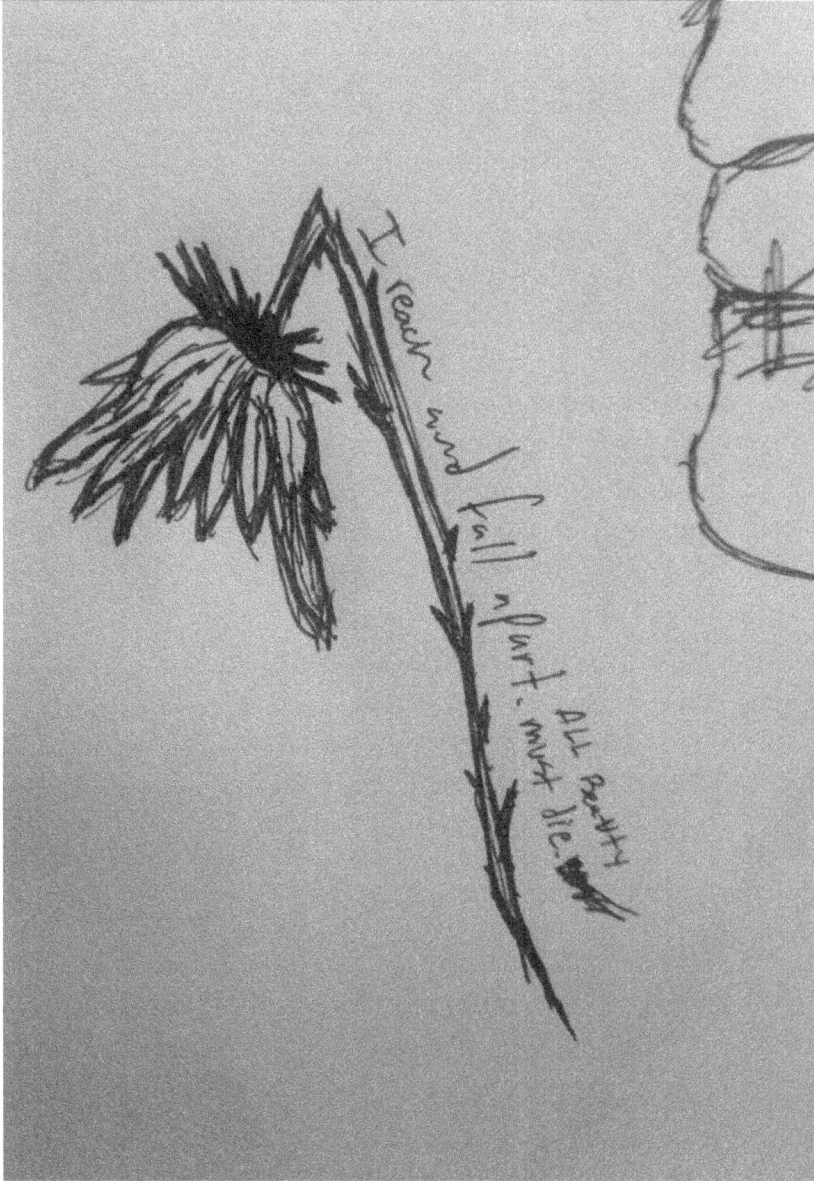

I reach and fall apart. ALL Beauty must die.

Born Ugly

Publically Personal Journal Entry no. 1

I write, or at least I attempt to. And not because I am willing to do so or want to all of the time as it can emotionally exhausting. Finding the right words to communicate whatever it is my head is looking to tell myself and the rest of the world takes a toll most non-artists wouldn't necessarily understand. And honestly it is never done as frequently as I would prefer it to be. Too often do I succumb to my selfish desires riddled with vanity and want what I post to hold up some sort of philosophical insight, meaning or merit to someone somewhere. Or at least let the ideas swelling inside my brain be heard out into vast space we consume. I joke on stage when I speak about how I am just looking for attention, and seeking the approval of others and it gets a laugh but its also not a joke at the same time. The vulnerably writing creates and trails behind reminds me of the discharge from freshly picked scab, the irritating sting that can be far too much to handle. Much like the songs I have sang, or may still try to sing, as my writing isn't limited just to a collection of words. But God dammit it all I am here again at the keyboard carelessly letting go and it's just because it's all I have ever known to do. The liquor and tobacco push themselves down and the words and songs just purge themselves about pouring without any sort of mercy or glory. The stench of what is rung from my lungs is genuine, and the bile it spills goes beyond my control.

At the end of it all however, throwing my vanity, wishful thinking, and love for an audience I just simply love words. I just do. It's why I have always written or done my best to write. It's music and song without notes. Simple sounds projected from the tongue can hold the weight of that of a tombstone on one man and on the other it can liberates him of that very same burden. The power in what we say can crumble a nation both outside ourselves and inside our minds. Speak loudly with urgency. Speak with potency and truth. Speak with silence and speak genuinely. Don't cheapen your words and don't exhaust yourself filling space just to be vocal. Words are weapons, be the champion marksmen.

Born Ugly

The End Is The Beginning Of The End

It all ends
It all begins
The bullet leaves the gun

Party lights go out
I smoke my lovers to the filter
The puddle dries in the sun

You run back to stay in place
The holes are filled
And we're back were we begun

Could our simple purpose, while it not being the grand reasoning of course, purely be that each of us are our experiments to nature in our own unique and individual way? That's the purpose of each creature as an individual and surely not the grand painting of all things within this master-or-disaster-piece?

Born Ugly

Too Young To Feel This Old

I shiver with the smoke
As the rain water drips
The bite of times vampire
Leaves me in its grips

The sounds of the earth
Another Inhale another toxic breath
Each passing second is a memory
And another closer to death

Embrace me
Take me
Hold me
Never let go

Minute's slips by
I still sit where I have always been
Waiting for the that final second
To never be brought back to where we began.

Born Ugly

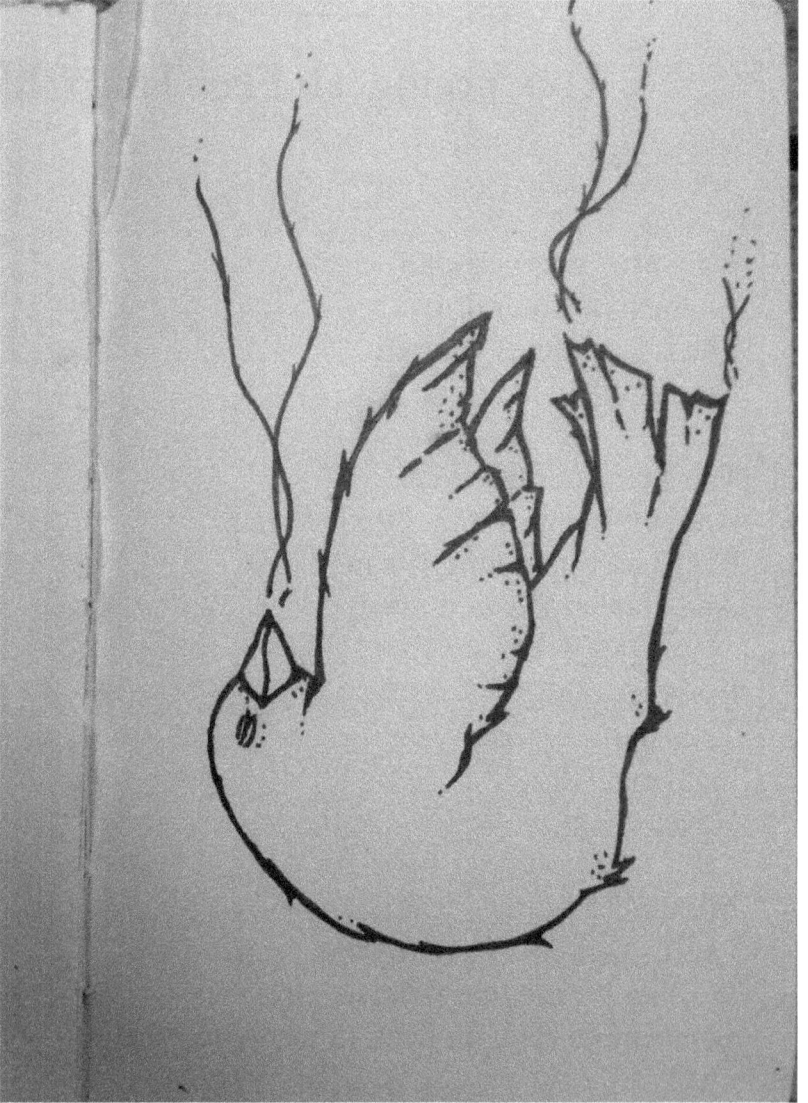

All In A Year

I hurt myself and I hurt others. A year of quiet and loud both cranked at ear shattering volumes. It was one where I started as confused as ever, achieved answers and concluded it with the distraught dissolution and lack of understanding I was once familiar with. Each year brings a new suffering and new satisfaction, new friends and new wars. The next may be the same but hopefully not one where I continue to believe I make two steps forward and then one step back only to see through it all I am just running in place.

Born Ugly

Personally Public Journal Entry No. 2

I don't know entirely know what else to say expect discomfort. I just feel a void and surrounding that void is pent up dissatisfaction with everything about my work and myself. I feel like I am doing something wrong or something's missing. Music doesn't always sound as good, it's sometimes hard to read or write and the quiet just outright terrifies me. People frighten me, even loved ones and yet I crave their approval like a dog in heat.

Sometimes you make life changes both minor and major but the various chord changes end result isn't the song you built it all up to be.

So the word of the day is dissatisfaction because that's what I have growing inside. Nothing more, nothing less.

Date an artist. Do it and start an ongoing cycle of complete misery and self-doubt. Just like them. Just like me.

An out of control train where the conductor is lost and that seems to never run out of track. And then one day the train hits a wall and the world moves forward.

Born Ugly

Cody Conrad

I don't believe in God
That's just an opiate
But I sure as hell believe in the devil.

He's in all of us
After the bottle hits the ground
And shatters.

A Tale of a Scorched Earth

Human beings have walked the earth to simply survive. Moving structures of calcium and flesh. Through time we have created buildings, temples, empires, and gods. We are now the gods we have made. The common necessity and practice of survival is surpassed by the desire of immortality; statues, monuments, documents, and the exploitation of the entire universe just to ensure our own place and preserve the power we believed to have had. That we were here, that we had risen above the elements and conquered beyond all that could conquer. And people of all walks of life have now inherit wish to simply be remembered. Lives of luxury, charisma, importance and property. This unintentional evolution has now made our selfishness an instinct engrained into our biological chemistry. But the sun knows not of such a personal wish, that of hedonism. It grows, and grows and grows. And all the while we kill and lie and cheat because we ourselves are not an apex predator, no we are gods. Disillusion has made us strong, and the heart weak. Humans all share one thing in common with themselves, and the Earth of which we walk upon and that's mortality. No statue or structure can stand and no book can stay bound. Even the sun lives on borrowed time. Nature is cruel and beautiful for there is rest in what it holds for all those who take a breath. In the end the oil we killed for will only lead us to become oil ourselves. Soon the sky will crack and the sun will swallow and consume like we have so then what will the human race have to show for years of malice, violence, and lust? Just simply ask the dust.

Born Ugly

11/6/14

On certain nights much like tonight I am swiftly reminded why I enjoy the company of records and books above other people. Records and books don't lash out at you, don't belittle you and don't bite back. They settle a weary soul.

Personally Public Journal Entry No. 3

You hate me. And when it's all over you may still feel the same. But I loved you from the beginning and when it's all over I will feel the same.

Born Ugly

Personally Public Journal Entry No. 4

As an artist I have learned it is wrong to have small moments of feeling good about ones self and ones work. I suppose it loses the majesty of mystery of the face behind the art itself. But if you know me at all you may know very well know that I am not the most mentally healthy person; many others are obviously far worse than I but never the less I have daily struggles with a variety of issues that that push me to cling on to various coping mechanisms both positive and negative.

I don't always try to read into negative or positive criticisms much these days, it can hurt the focus of my work, but on occasion I take a glance and the last few days I have received uplifting messages and insights that my work isn't all that bad like I sometimes feel it is. Those small senses of euphoria are encouraging so I bask in it for a brief moment in time and than back at it I go to the grind. Upon reviewing these encouraging criticisms with a select group of close friends and artists. Some however pushed me to not take to heart any acclaim, and although I agree to an extent right now I am saying "fuck it". With the struggles I have and the strides I have made forward through them I don't see it wrong to taste the honey drip of these pleasurable messages. So to those I say thank you.

It's only a matter of time anyway before my brain checks itself back into the hole self discouragement and with control I will allow it to push me. I do what I do within my abilities, which isn't much, however I can't take it any further aside from growth through time. I'll do what I do and not care to think about the opposed, the naysayers or critics, and especially to those who question my personal joy that I reached out on a whim and gave another a feeling of relation or life from my work. If you don't like what I do I say take it as your own and do it better than myself.

Back to work.

Born Ugly

Personally public journal entry no. 5

   The last two years have been a very serious trial for me. Being hurt and hurting others. I have severed ties that may never be sewn back together and made enough mistakes to fill a college text book; all rooted in selfishness and anger. I long for vindication but the ghosts of the past still linger and weigh on my back like that of a tombstone. I feel embarrassed to the person I once was and who I still sometimes come back to. They say you shouldn't live with regrets but I do. A countless number of them in fact. But I suppose I keep moving forward, learning, reaching and growing even with a heavy heart that may never become lighter. It's either that or die.
So to those who have felt pain inflicted by me I am truly sorry. And to those who hurt me I forgive you.

Tin Can Coffin

You can rob me of my home
My material goods
Break my heart
Take my loved ones
And crush my dignity to bits.

But through all the violence
And all the heartache
I still have the inevitable peace
That is the grave.
That can never be stolen.

Born Ugly

The days are dry
My skin is a whore
The bottle flows
Whiskey
Leaks
From
These
Open
Sores

Blood is believed to be thicker than water.
But wine is greater than both combined.

Born Ugly

"Howls for the lonely cannibal"

I don't wish to wait
Yet here I sit
Waiting for those returned calls

I kept quiet for so long
But how quiet can a coyote be
When it's preys been when lying
Dead for so long
Singing its dying song

The howls and whistles ring
While I await amongst the pack
To feast on what's been dead
Before my lonely harvest

A pure blessing
You're not what I deserved
Drifting from my appetite
But regardless I'll wait.

Despite desperate longing
And what I deserve isn't
What lies before
But I am sorry.

Cody Conrad

Smile, you're responsible

It's hit. Adulthood. Of course it's been there for a while but what I am referring to is something different. And Although the photo above of myself may say otherwise in regards to my coming of age into adulthood it has occurred to me officially that I am truly of the age where my peers have careers, graduated from their respective universities, gotten married and are preparing for children, or have had them. What follows next for these fellow pupils of mine now is growing into themselves as established adults in a functioning working society. A purgatory of sorts until the crash of middle age and the crisis that is leeched on to it. However I am wondering where this leaves me. As I have chosen a different path of those in the normal and functioning world. I feel that if I found myself traveling down the average path I would just end it all on my deathbed with my final dying breath being "so that was it?". But than again I say that now and I am only 23. When will any of us say "this truly is it" with absolute certainty and what is "it" after all? I clearly can recall myself as a young boy in elementary school having the thought and excitement that I just couldn't wait until I would be exactly 22. For whatever reason that number in my head represented wisdom, freedom, being young but being set with both your life and self. Now the joke is on me. I have only bred more questions in my growing years than what I had as a young adolescent. Every action of myself and others around the globe opens an ever widening wormhole of thought,

Born Ugly

inquisition, confusion and very little resolution.

       I guess so far I know one thing for certain and that's that we occupy, for now, a 1,000 trillion metric ton rock called Earth. And on Earth we have a life given that just seems to be an endless and aimless run around of finding what pieces fit our puzzle, and discovering what we really just don't like at all.

I love words. It's why I have always written. It's music and song without notes. Simple sounds projected from the tongue can hold the weight of that of a tombstone on one man and on the other it can liberates him of that very same burden. The power in what we say can crumble a nation both outside ourselves and inside our minds. Speak loudly with urgency. Speak with potency and truth. Speak with silence and speak genuinely. Don't cheapen your words and don't exhaust yourself filling space just to be vocal. Words are weapons, be the champion marksmen.

Born Ugly

My own death isn't what scares me but witnessing someone in their final days and knowing their life is now behind them leaves me shivering and terrified.

Each year we make it through we passed a day and time that belongs to us, a forth-coming anniversary of mortality. And soon the date will arrive and all I could ever want to say to you will be clogged in the passageway of my heart and mouth by crippling heartache. I feel it in my bones as it comes closer; all I want to say is I love you and thank you.

People are more than time, even after they give their last breath, last step and final words, something lasts in someone somewhere. And there lies immortality.

Cody Conrad

Born Ugly

If post industrial revolution man would kill all the insects that live on the Earth, it will die along with them.

If all humans perish then the earth will flourish once again as it should be.

For me there's freedom in a storm. It's almost like for a single second the world I walk upon is in sync with what goes on within my own head. And in those moments I find solace and love with the internal tug of war as it is not just me that screams but 6,000,000,000,000,000,000,000,000 kilograms of rock.

Grave of the Fireflies

The grave in its grace is so benign,
As ashes grow the field with the passage of time.
The grave in its grace is so divine,
As ashes grow the wound with the passage of time.

A box, in a fold
A tin made to hold
Your loved ones.
Hungry, and high
From not sleeping at night
Bathed in filth
A war, a fight
Beneath opium skies
Leaves you skeletal
But a boy, or a man
Will not except hands
Coveted by charity.

Dissonance.

Clarity.

Vacant bodies.

The Crib Death of Cody Conrad

I've seen mermaids
I've seen Loch Ness
I've seen God
I believe in what's already been gone

Who wants to die?

I've seen the Sun burn
But your face is a distant figure
Now take me to your gates
Prove me wrong

I want to die!

Take me to the crow
Mouth full of feathers
I pray I've been wrong
I pray this just wasn't my voice
Bouncing off the walls and back to me

Born Ugly

Melting House of Sin

Let the ringing in my ears
Be the ringing of your voice

I hear the footsteps of phantoms
The hallways creek with their movements
Of time and memory

A wet dream of sound in my head
And nothing more than scribbles
On the mental photographs clung to the walls
Of my mind

The house stands with your prints
As I sit on the cold tile floor always waiting for
That ring to make its way home again

I leave you with this:

Write what hurts. Write when you can't. Write when you don't want to. Write in moments of when you're faint. Write when you bleed. Write when you breathe. Write when you've had too much to drink. Write when there's nothing coming to mind. Write in despair. Write when it means nothing. Write because maybe through the nonsense you'll find something worth noting.

Born Ugly

Over these passed few years through heartache, loss
empty bottles and utter shipwreck I have become
calloused to ever expect goodwill from anyone.
Becoming jaded and cynical at such a ripe age
was never the goal but alas here I sit.
Nevertheless I have encountered individuals as of late
that pushed throughtnat hardness , or I have taken
notice to some who stood there all along.
To get to the point I am typing these words as a
simple thanksto those whostill show me kindness
despite my very many and often reoccurring short
comings. And in this search of clarity I have
now learned one important thing: I cannot change
the wind but I can control my sails.

CC

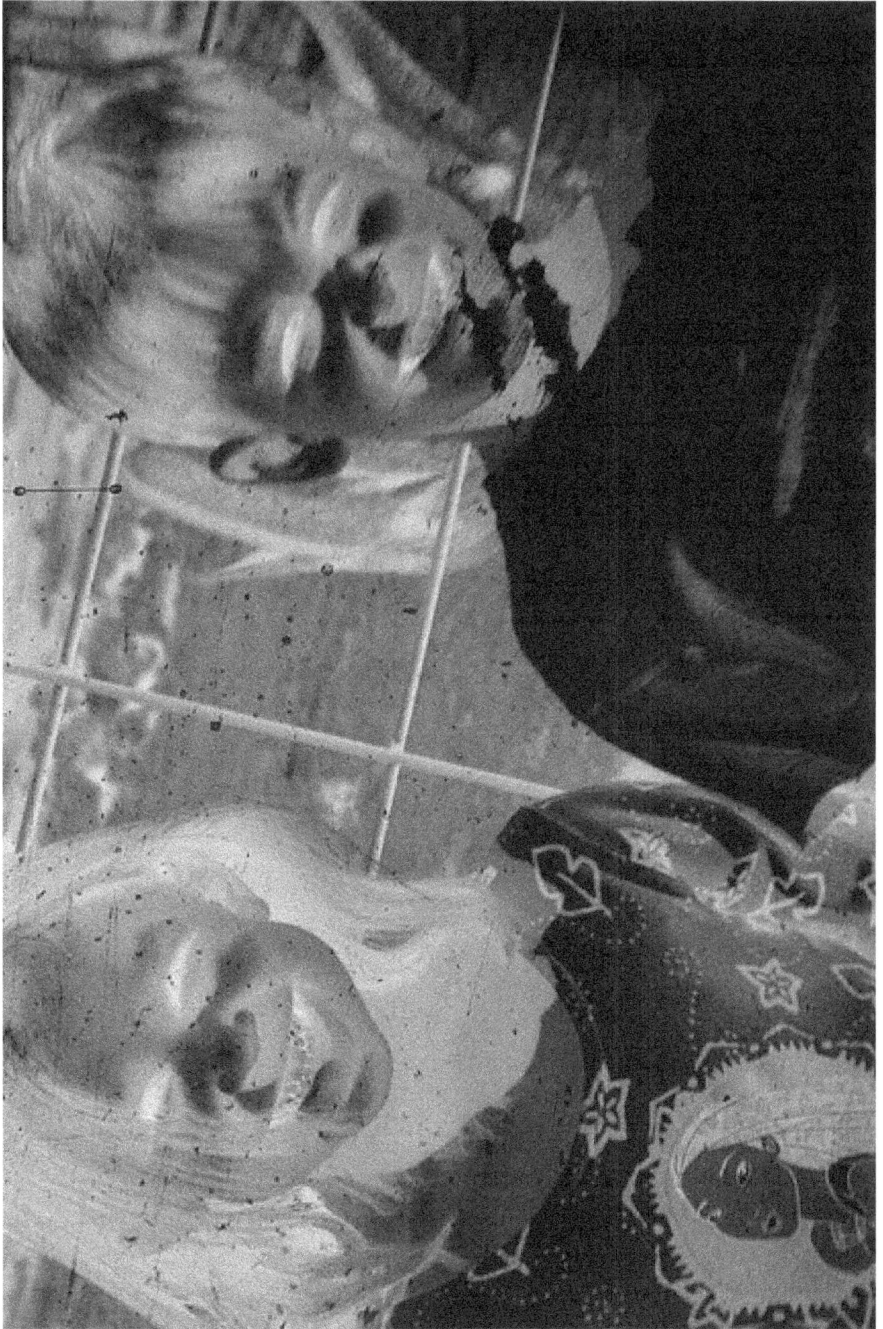

Born Ugly

Born Ugly

About the Author

Cody Conrad is an active touring musician, writer, stand up/speaker, visual artist, multi media explorer, social activist and ritually attempts to practice all things DIY to any capacity, such as this book you are holding now.

For more of his work as far as music, writing, speaking, charitable work or shows visit newfleshpress.com.

And for praises or grievances he can reached at newfleshpress@gmail.com

Cody Conrad

Born Ugly

www.ingramcontent.com/pod-product-compliance
Lightning Source LLC
Chambersburg PA
CBHW020950030426
42339CB00004B/40